The W Mercy Explained

By Silvia Vecchini

Illustrated by Antonio Vincenti

Pauline
BOOKS & MEDIA
Boston

Contents

The Works of Mercy

The works of mercy have a long tradition in the Church. From the earliest days Christians have reached out with these works to widows, orphans, prisoners, and all people in any kind of need. Over the centuries the works of mercy have inspired great saints, witnesses, and founders of religious orders. They have always been closely tied to what the Gospel proclaims and what the sacraments signify. It could not be otherwise. But what exactly are the works of mercy? And what does it mean to put them into practice? We begin by taking a closer look at a very interesting word.

Mercy

What does the word "mercy" mean?

It comes from the Latin word *misericordia*, which is a combination of **misereor (to have pity or compassion) and cor (heart)**. Together these two words express the idea of a heartfelt compassion for others—one that pushes us to help, to understand, and to forgive.

In the Bible, the two Hebrew words that are associated with mercy are *rahamim* and *hesed*. **Rahamim** literally means "entrails" and often refers to a mother's womb. This word points to the intimate and special bond between mother and child. The closeness of this kind of relationship permits one to feel the joy and pain of the other as if it were one's own.

Hesed on the other hand speaks of an alliance that is characterized by fidelity and love. This is the kind of love that God has for his people—a love that is undeserved, eternal, unfailing, and kind.

Mercy, therefore, is a trait that involves the heart. It is seeing others with tenderness, but also with a desire and willingness to act for their good.

God Is Merciful

Mercy is a trait, a characteristic of God. Numerous Bible passages teach us about God's mercy. In Exodus, God proclaims that he is: "The LORD, the LORD, a God merciful and gracious, slow to anger, and abounding in steadfast love and faithfulness" (Ex 34:6). Later, in the New Testament, Jesus reveals the forgiving love of God. The parable of the Prodigal Son, found in Luke 15:11–32, is also known as the parable of the Merciful Father.

Mercy isn't just reserved for God alone. He invites us to be like him. In the Gospel, Jesus personally invites each one of us to **"be merciful, just as your Father is merciful"** (Lk 6:36).

Pope Francis' Desire

Our Pope wants us to rediscover God's mercy. That is why Pope Francis called for an Extraordinary Jubilee Year of Mercy. Saint Thomas Aquinas taught that mercy is a quality of God and that it is in his mercy that God shows his almighty power.

How can this be? Kindness is often mistaken for weakness in our world. But mercy is not a weakness—**it is the strength of God's love**! Through mercy, God loves us unconditionally and *never* ceases to forgive and renew us.

Pope Francis wants the faithful to fall in love with God's mercy, tenderness, and love. Because of this love, we are called to love our neighbor. And as Saint John of the Cross wrote: "In the evening of life, we will be judged on love."

Pope Francis recommends that Christians reflect on both the corporal and spiritual works of mercy. He suggests that this is a way to reawaken **our sleeping consciences** and to enter more deeply into the heart of the Gospel. The Holy Father invites us to encounter the poor the way Jesus did. Pope Francis reminds us that it was Jesus who gave us the works of mercy so that we could know whether or not we are living as his disciples.

Corporal Works of Mercy

Feed the hungry.
Give drink to the thirsty.
Clothe the naked.
Shelter the homeless.
Visit the sick.
Visit the imprisoned.
Bury the dead.

Spiritual Works of Mercy

Counsel the doubtful.
Instruct the ignorant.
Admonish the sinner.
Comfort the afflicted.
Forgive offenses willingly.
Bear wrongs patiently.
Pray for the living and the dead.

In his message of September 1, 2016, Pope Francis proposed a new work of mercy:

Care for our common home (the earth)

This includes all that we do to take care of the environment, avoid pollution, and preserve our natural resources.

We begin our discovery of the works of mercy so that they can be imprinted in our hearts and show us the way. Words from Scripture, the saints, and Pope Francis will guide us.

As we move ahead you will also find **Notebook** pages; these are spaces for your thoughts and questions. There are reflections on these pages that can help you consider what you have read.

Corporal Works of Mercy

1. Feed the Hungry

"The fasting
I want, is it not
to share your bread
with the hungry?"

See Is 58:6–7

1st   Daily Bread

In the prayer that Jesus taught us, the **Our Father**, we say: "Give us this day our daily bread." With these words we ask God to provide for our material needs, those things that help us live each day. As we pray, we ask for ourselves and intercede for all men and women. We are united to those who are suffering and recognize the needs of all our brothers and sisters.

If we want to carry out this first work of mercy, prayer alone is not enough. God asks us to provide for our neighbor, to intervene where there is a need, to share our "bread" with others. But what do we mean by "bread"? It means all food, the sustenance necessary for survival that should not be denied to anyone.

In the world there are many people who are hungry and don't have enough to eat—many of them are children. Without sufficient food they cannot grow and become strong and healthy adults; some even die from malnutrition and starvation. Yet in some parts of the world,

Many of the works of mercy can be found in Gospel passages in which Jesus speaks of the end times and the final judgment.

"When the Son of Man comes in his glory, and all the angels with him, then he will sit on the throne of his glory. All the nations will be gathered before him, and he will separate people one from another as a shepherd separates the sheep from the goats, and he will put the sheep at his right hand and the goats at the left. Then the king will say to those at his right hand, 'Come you that are blessed by my Father, inherit the kingdom prepared for you from the foundation of the world; **for I was hungry and you gave me food, I was thirsty and you gave me something to drink, I was a stranger and you welcomed me, I was naked and you gave me**

people waste food every day. This is unjust. Feeding the hungry challenges us to do something for those who lack the food they need. It also calls us to reflect on whether or not we are wasting the food we have.

This work of mercy urges us to **give our neighbors what they need to live**—and not to turn away. It also asks us to understand even deeper hungers. A person can be starving for love and understanding and *that* is the "bread" they need from us. The first work of mercy reminds us that in the Eucharist Jesus becomes the living Bread for us. He is the food that satisfies our hunger for love, for life, and for eternity: "I am the living bread that came down from heaven. Whoever eats of this bread will live forever . . ." (Jn 6:51). When we allow Jesus to feed us, we become more like him. Then our lives can become "bread": gift and sustenance for others.

Jesus' Words

clothing, I was sick and you took care of me, I was in prison and you visited me.' Then the righteous will answer him, 'Lord, when was it that we saw you hungry and gave you food, or thirsty and gave you something to drink? And when was it that we saw you a stranger and welcomed you, or naked and gave you clothing? And when was it that we saw you sick or in prison and we visited you?' And the king will answer them, 'Truly I tell you, just as you did it to one of the least of these who are members of my family, you did it to me.' Then he will say to those at his left hand, 'You that are accursed, depart from me into the eternal fire prepared for the devil and his angels; for I was hungry and you gave me no food, I was thirsty and you gave me nothing to drink, I was a stranger and you did not welcome me, naked and you did not give me clothing, sick and in prison and you did not visit me.' Then they also will answer, 'Lord, when was it that we saw you hungry or thirsty or a stranger or naked or sick or in prison, and did not take care of you?' Then he will answer them, **'Truly I tell you, just as you did not do it to one of the least of these, you did not do it to me'** (Mt 25:31–45).

Notebook

✓ Ask yourself how you care for the life of your neighbors. Reflect on the ways you can provide for your neighbors' needs. Look around: What "bread" do those who are near you need? What are your siblings, your friends, your classmates hungry for? Write below what you can do to feed them.

. . . .

. . . .

. . . .

. . . .

✓ Mother Teresa spent her life serving the poor and the marginalized by caring for their physical and spiritual needs. Ask God to show you one person you can "feed" today.

> "Hunger for love is much more difficult to satisfy than hunger for bread."
>
> Attributed to Mother Teresa of Calcutta

✓ There are many programs and initiatives that aim at giving food to people who don't have enough to eat. Together with your friends and your parish, you can organize something to help the poor. You can collect money or non-perishable items to help keep parish outreach ministries, local food pantries, or soup kitchens stocked. You may ask your parents about offering to pay for someone else's groceries when your family is shopping. Your class may prepare baskets or bags of food to give away and decorate them with a word or phrase from the Gospel.

Corporal Works of Mercy

2. Give Drink to the Thirsty

"Everyone who thirsts, come to the Water . . ."

Is 55:1

Water for Life

Our bodies need both food and water. The lack of water, however, will kill a person long before the lack of food can. Water is indispensable for life, and yet in the world more than a billion people do not have access to drinkable water. There are even more people who get their drinking water from unhealthy sources that expose them to various diseases. Not even animals or plants can live without adequate water. **Life is not possible without water.** That's why the United Nations declared that access to water is a human right.

Jesus, True Source

Jesus is the Savior sent by God the Father so that men and women receive "water," that is, love. Here is what the evangelist John wrote:

"So [Jesus] came to a Samaritan city called Sychar, near the plot of ground that Jacob had given to his son, Joseph. Jacob's well was there, and Jesus, tired out by his journey, was sitting by the well. It was about noon.

"A Samaritan woman came to draw water, and Jesus said to her, 'Give me a drink.' (His disciples had gone to the city to buy food.) The Samaritan woman said to him, 'How is it that you, a Jew, ask a drink of me, a woman of Samaria?' (Jews do not share their things with Samaritans.) Jesus answered her, 'If you knew the gift of

Along with the first work of mercy, to which this one is closely tied, we are called to do everything in our power to assure that those who are thirsty can drink and that all who need water can access it. Water is a resource that all people must share in a just manner, as brothers and sisters would, without overusing it or excluding anyone. This work of mercy also urges us to reflect on how we use water each day and to ask ourselves whether we are being responsible with it.

Jesus was born in a land where water was drawn from wells every day by women and children using heavy buckets—a method of getting water that's still used in many parts of the world today. That is why Jesus was inspired to speak of a gushing spring of water: the Holy Spirit, **which is always capable of quenching our deepest thirsts.** As usual Jesus calls us to do more. He reminds us that the world is "thirsty" for love, and that those who know God's love can quench their neighbor's thirst and offer themselves freely to others.

God, and who it is that is saying to you, "Give me a drink," you would have asked him, and he would have given you living water.' The woman said to him, 'Sir, you have no bucket, and the well is deep. Where do you get that living water? Are you greater than our ancestor Jacob, who gave us the well, and with his sons and his flocks drank from it?' Jesus said to her, 'Everyone who drinks of this water will be thirsty again, but those who drink of the water that I will give them will never be thirsty. The water that I will give will become in them a spring of water gushing up to eternal life'" (Jn 4:5–14).

Notebook

v Mother Teresa spent her life among the poorest of the poor in India. Her example reminds you that when you "quench" someone's thirst, you are freely choosing to love your neighbor. When you give what you yourself need, you also receive a gift: your own thirst is quenched.

Think of a time when someone gave you "water" to drink. How are you being invited to do the same for others?

"Lord,
when I am hungry,
give me someone who has need of food.
When I am thirsty,
send me someone who has need of a drink.
When I am cold,
send me someone to warm.
When I am disappointed,
offer me someone to console."

Attributed to Mother Teresa of Calcutta

v Think of your daily actions. Do you waste water?

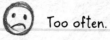 Too often.

 Hardly ever.

 Only sometimes.

 Never!

Corporal Works of Mercy

3. Clothe the Naked

"*The necessities of life are water, bread, and clothing, and also a house to assure privacy.*"

Sir 29:21

Nakedness

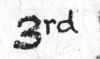

We are born small, fragile, and naked. We possess nothing. We depend on our families to clothe us, help us, and feed us. This dependence is true for all of us and for all our lives. We all depend on God; we also depend on one another.

In the Bible, nudity is a sign of our **dependence**; our poverty; and our need to be protected, loved, and cared for. We may not be aware that there are those near us who need to be "clothed." If we look around

A Gesture That Still Speaks Today

Do you know the story of Saint Martin of Tours? He was born in 316 in Upper Pannonia (modern-day Hungary and Slovenia) to pagan parents. His father, an officer in the Roman army, was called to serve in northern Italy. Martin learned about Christianity there, but was not baptized. Martin became a soldier when he was still young. His name is connected to a famous gesture that signaled the decisive moment of his conversion.

When Martin was stationed in Gaul (modern-day France), he had an experience that became the hallmark of his life. As Martin stood at the entrance of the city with his soldiers, he encountered a shivering beggar in tattered clothes. Feeling compassion for the man, Martin tore his military cape in two and gave one half to him. Then Martin wrapped himself in the other half and continued on his way.

we see store clothing displays that are constantly changing. Our closets and drawers may be full—so much so that we may have to make space for any new clothes.

The third work of mercy reminds us that this is not the case for everyone. Many people are so poor that they really do have nothing to wear. Things that are extra for us **may be needed** by someone else.

That is why there are so many groups that collect clothes for poor people all over the world. Through these initiatives we can give new or used clothing that is in good condition to others so that they can live with more dignity.

That night Martin dreamed that Jesus Christ came to him dressed in the half of the cloak that Martin had given to the beggar. He heard Jesus say to the angels surrounding him, "Here is Martin, the Roman soldier who is not baptized; he clothed me." The dream had such an impact on him that Martin decided to be baptized the following day. Martin spent the rest of his life in service to others as a monk near the city of Tours.

On the 1600th anniversary of Martin's death, Pope Saint John Paul II reminded us that **Saint Martin is an important witness to charity because he translated Jesus' words into action**.

Notebook

✓ Giving away clothes you don't need is something you can do for people you've never met before as well as those you know. It is easy to put clothing in a donation box. But when giving something to someone you know personally, it is necessary to respect the person's dignity. Think of some ways to be gentle and sensitive to the feelings of those you help.

✓ Circle the answer that best represents your answer. Do you demand particular brands or articles of clothing?

 Often. I really like expensive or beautiful clothing!

Hardly ever.

 Only a few times.

 Never! As long as it's clean and appropriate, the kind of clothing I wear isn't that important to me.

✓ Read the selection below from an ancient Christian author. Discuss with a friend or family member how to involve your parish, school, or neighborhood in a clothing drive.

"If one undresses a person who is clothed they are called a thief. And the one who doesn't clothe the naked when he is able to do so, does that person deserve another name? The bread you have for yourself is also for the hungry; the cloak that you keep safely in your wardrobe belongs to the naked; the shoes that rot in your house belong to those who have none; the silver that you are saving underground belongs to the needy."

Saint Basil the Great

Corporal Works of Mercy

4. Shelter the Homeless

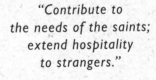

"Contribute to the needs of the saints; extend hospitality to strangers."

Rom 12:13

Welcoming the Pilgrim

The definition of "pilgrim" is a person on a **journey toward a specific place, often a holy place**. A pilgrim wants to go to a place of worship where a person can return to God and grow closer to him.

Over the centuries many Christians have gone on pilgrimages to the Holy Land—the places where Jesus lived and preached. Christians also go to places dear to Christian tradition and tied to the saints, martyrs, or the Blessed Mother. Because these journeys exposed pilgrims to danger, exhaustion, and many long days of walking, giving shelter to pilgrims was—and is—considered an important work of mercy by Christians.

But who are today's "pilgrims"?

Certainly there are still people who go on religious pilgrimages with the intention of living their faith more profoundly. But there are other people we can consider "pilgrims."

In many countries hundreds and hundreds of refugees arrive every day. **Many are fleeing their homelands because of war, famine, and conditions of extreme poverty.**

The practice of hospitality, however, is even more ancient than Christianity. **Welcoming and respecting the "stranger"** who is away from his homeland is visible throughout the Old Testament. The people of Israel—God's chosen people—had the painful experience of being foreigners, or "aliens," in Egypt, far from the land God had given them. In Egypt they were exploited and oppressed. God remembers his people and asks them to remember their own experience: "You shall not wrong or oppress a resident alien, for you were aliens in the land of Egypt" (Ex 22:21), and also: "The alien who resides with you shall be to you as the citizen among you; you shall love the alien as yourself" (Lev 19:34).

Today's Pilgrims

At great risk to themselves they crossed desserts, seas, rivers, mountains, and all kinds of terrain because their lives at home were being threatened.

On the occasion of the World Day of Refugees, Pope Francis invited all of us to ask for forgiveness on behalf of anyone who closes the door on those who are searching for a family, or who need to be taken care of. He encouraged us to respect the dignity of our brothers and sisters who are far from home and to pray for all who are seeking refuge where they can live without fear.

If we consider ourselves Christians, we must think about how to give hospitality to today's pilgrims and welcome those who have nothing or are escaping famine, war, and death.

Notebook

∨ Giving hospitality means opening one's heart, one's life, perhaps even one's home to those who need to be welcomed. Everyone can do something. How can you "open" your "door" to make room for someone?

New family members, friends, classmates, teammates, neighbors, teachers, and pastors: all these people long to be welcomed. Write down a time you remember when you hoped someone would welcome you.

> "We have all known the long loneliness, and we have learned that the only solution is love and that love comes with community."
>
> Servant of God Dorothy Day

> "Do not neglect to show hospitality to strangers, for by doing that some have entertained angels without knowing it."
>
> Hebrews 13:2

∨ Are you welcoming toward others?

Are you quick to listen to those who are close to you?

Are you able at times to put the needs of another person before your own?

Corporal Works of Mercy

5. Visit the Sick

"Do not hesitate
to visit the sick,
because for such deeds
you will be loved."

Sir 7:35

The Gift That Returns

"Why me? What did I do to deserve this?"

Sometimes, when we are sick, we experience a sense of loss or loneliness. Sometimes, we may even feel angry.

This work of mercy touches all of us closely because we know that we ourselves may become sick. Many of us have had the experience of someone at home or one of our friends being seriously ill or in a hospital for medical treatment or recovery.

The Christian practice of visiting the sick is truly ancient. In fact, one of the first things the Church did when Christianity was made legal in the Roman Empire was to build a hospital in every city in which there was a cathedral. Today, too, the Church is still building hospitals in every part of the world in order to make surgery, medical treatment, and medications available to all.

The fifth work of mercy invites us to respond personally. It urges us to **open our eyes and hearts** to the suffering of those who

Jesus says, "I will restore you."

Christians learn to pay attention to the ill, the suffering, and the most fragile from Jesus himself.

Throughout the Gospels, we see that even in the midst of the crowd, Jesus never backed away when those who were suffering reached out for him. Remember that in Jesus' time people thought there was a link between suffering and guilt. They believed that illness was the consequence of sin committed either by the person who was ill or by his family members or ancestors. The weight of shame made sickness in those times need treatment and comfort, support, or simply our company. To "visit" the sick means to be with them (at home or in the hospital); it means to give them our presence, our full attention, and our warmth and affection. Visiting the sick is a way to express our closeness and compassion with generosity.

The word **compassion** means "suffering with." When we have compassion for others, we are attentive to their pain in a personal way and want to help make it more bearable.

The first thing to do for someone who is injured or ill is to make ourselves available to listen. Listening attentively and patiently to what a person wishes to share, even when it isn't pleasant, can actually relieve suffering.

When we give of ourselves to visit a neighbor who is injured or ill, we also receive something. The moment our neighbor tells us his doubts and questions, or she shares her difficulties and hopes, we become participants in that person's situation. We receive the gift of moving beyond ourselves, and our eyes are opened to fragility and pain. This gift is precious because it is an opportunity to **grow in our humanity** and our faith.

an even greater burden to carry. Those who had contagious diseases were marginalized and avoided. Often, they were not permitted to work even if they were able to do so. Many would have no choice but to beg for money.

Jesus always made himself available to suffering people. He entered the homes of those who were ill; he touched lepers; he stopped to speak with those who sat in the dust along his way; he healed even on the Sabbath day. Jesus made people whole, comforted them, and gave them the strength they needed to stand.

Jesus still heals the sick today, sometimes miraculously and sometimes through good medicine. But he comes to us with a deeper kind of healing, one that concerns every person regardless of his state of health—the healing of the heart.

In the Gospels, we read: "Come to me, all you that are weary and are carrying heavy burdens, and I will give you rest" (Mt 11:28).

Notebook

✓ Read this text by an ancient Christian author who reminds us that we all need Jesus to be our Savior, shepherd, teacher, and more. Underline the words that draw you to feel united to those who suffer illness or invite you to bring comfort and help when you are able to do so.

"We who are ill
  are in need of the Savior.
We, the lost, need a guide.
We, the blind, need the one who carries the light.
We, the thirsty, need him
  who is the font of life
so that our thirst may be completely quenched.
We, the dead, need life.
We, the sheep, need the shepherd,
  and children need teachers.
In summary, all of our human existence
  needs Christ."

Saint Clement of Alexandria

✓ Collect information on the ways your parish reaches out to those who are ill. Put a check next to the initiatives on the list below that currently exist. With your family or religious education class, choose a way to contribute to the activities already being done or think of a new one.

☐ Healing ministry or offering the Sacrament of the Sick

☐ Periodic visits to the sick of the parish

☐ Helping those with disabilities (shopping, yard work, etc.)

☐ Rides for the elderly

☐ Other . . .

Corporal Works of Mercy

6. Visit the Imprisoned

"Remember those who are in prison, as though you were in prison with them; those who are being tortured, as though you yourselves were being tortured."

Heb 13:3

Without Judging

The sixth work of mercy invites us to remember those who are serving time in prison.

This work of mercy is important, because it brings a strong light into the depths of our hearts so that we may see whether feelings of fear and judgment are hidden there. It makes us ask ourselves: How do we view criminals who have been incarcerated? Do we judge them? It is simplistic to divide people into two categories, good and evil. And while God's law helps us to judge whether an **action** is right or wrong, no one has given us the authority to judge other **people**.

Prison inmates have made wrong decisions. They have fallen to temptation and committed crimes. They are suffering the consequences of their choices and are paying the price for their deeds in a cell, without freedom, without their families, and without their personal possessions. **Our judgments don't help** convicts.

While it is necessary that they serve their sentences, society should

Shortly after his election as the new pope, Pope Francis chose to visit a prison and celebrate Holy Thursday Mass with the inmates there. By doing this, the Holy Father reminded us that Jesus himself had been arrested and imprisoned on the night before he died.

At Mass, the Pope washed the feet of twelve male and female prisoners and brought the prisoners this powerful sign of God's love behind bars. On that occasion he told them that Jesus loves them without limit—there's always more love. The Holy Father also reminded them that God never gets assure that prisoners can do so in a way that **respects their dignity** as human beings. In addition, they should be provided with what is needed to help them rebuild their lives. Unfortunately there are many overcrowded prisons where many prisoners sink into hopelessness or become angry with themselves and aggressive toward others. The Church has numerous initiatives to care for prisoners so that they are given the **comfort and courage** they need to turn away from rage, desperation, and emptiness.

God in the Cell

tired of loving or forgiving anyone. God loves us all and God loved us so much that he gave his life for us. Pope Francis added that when Jesus gave his life for each of us, it means that he gave his life for you, for the Holy Father—for every one of us by name. Pope Francis affirmed that God's love is *personal* and that it never fades.

Recently the Holy Father reminded prison chaplains that the gestures and words that come from their hearts tell prisoners that the Lord does not remain outside their cells or outside the prison walls. Pope Francis wants convicts to know that God is in prison—crying, working, and waiting with each prisoner.

Notebook

V Saint John Bosco was a priest in Turin, Italy, in the 1800s. He often went to visit boys who found themselves in jail because they had stolen or committed other crimes. Many of these boys were poor, orphaned, or outcast. Read Don Bosco's thoughts below and then try to put his "formula" into practice today.

"Being good is not about avoiding sin or failure—oh no! Unfortunately, we fail and commit sins. Being good consists in this: in having the will to change.

"I want to give you the formula for holiness—first: being happy and at peace with God and others; second: being faithful to the duties of study and prayer; third: doing good to everyone around us."

Saint John Bosco

V Have you ever stopped to think what it takes to be merciful toward others' mistakes?

V Do you know how to forgive and give second chances to those who are close to you?

V Sometimes indifference, selfishness, or laziness make us "prisoners", they don't allow us to be truly free. Write down who and what makes you truly free in the space below.

....

....

Corporal Work of Mercy

7. Bury the Dead

"My child,
let your tears fall
for the dead, and as one
in great pain begin the lament.
Lay out the body with
due ceremony,
and do not neglect
the burial."

Sir 38:16

Water and Incense

Centuries ago there were many who did not have the means to bury their loved ones properly. Often bodies were abandoned and left unburied. That's why many religious organizations were founded with the intention of giving poor people a dignified burial after they died.

Today these associations serve others by praying for the deceased and participating in funeral rituals.

This last corporal work of mercy invites us to respect and care for those nearing the end of their lives. It also encourages us to reflect on the love that ought to accompany our memories of and prayers for our loved ones who have died.

The rites of Christian burial and commendation are rich in their references to eternal life. Pain and loss do not disappear, but we can walk through them strongly affirmed in our **belief in the resurrection**.

During the rites, the body of a deceased person is sprinkled with holy water as a remembrance of his or her Baptism. The body is also incensed to highlight the person's dignity and sacredness as a child of God. As Saint Paul reminds us: "Your body is a temple of the Holy Spirit within you" (1 Cor 6:19). For Christians death is a passage, a **return to the Father** who created us for eternal life.

Tobit Breaks the Law

In the Bible we read the story of Tobit, the only one who refused to worship idols that had been introduced to Israel by an evil king. Despite the insults and schemes of his neighbors, Tobit

Words of Prayer

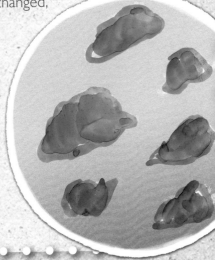

remained faithful. He continued to follow God's law and fulfill all its requirements including pilgrimages, helping the poor, and giving one tenth of his earnings to the temple. Even when Tobit was exiled to the city of Nineveh or difficult things happened to him, his family, or his people, Tobit stayed true to his faith.

Then the king of Nineveh had many Jewish people killed and would not allow anyone to bury them. He also commanded that anyone who did not follow this order would be condemned to death.

Tobit disobeyed the king's law because it was unjust. He knew that if he was forced to make a choice, following God's law was more important. He went out every night to retrieve the bodies and give them a dignified burial.

Even though he risked being discovered and had to flee for his life, Tobit refused to exempt himself from this work of compassion and profound humanity.

Notebook

✓ Read these words and reflect.

"Blessed be the God and Father of our Lord Jesus Christ! By his great mercy he has given us a new birth into a living hope through the resurrection of Jesus Christ from the dead, and into an inheritance that is imperishable, undefiled, and unfading, kept in heaven for you."

1 Peter 1:3-4

"For since we believe that Jesus died and rose again, even so, through Jesus, God will bring with him those who have died."

1 Thessalonians 4:14

✓ Look up the Nicene or Apostles' Creed. Write below the part of the Creed that talks about eternal life.

. . . .

. . . .

. . . .

✓ Do you truly believe in eternal life?

Spiritual Works of Mercy

1. Counsel the Doubtful

"I bless the LORD who gives me counsel; in the night also my heart instructs me. I keep the LORD always before me; because he is at my right hand, I shall not be moved."

Ps 16:7–8

A Perfect Counselor

It's not at all easy to give good advice or to find someone whose wisdom we can trust completely.

Whoever is doubtful or uncertain and seeks answers ought to be prudent and carefully choose a trustworthy guide. In the same way, whoever finds himself in a position of giving counsel ought to do it without self-interest, without receiving anything in return, and seeking the good of the other person.

This first spiritual work of mercy encourages us to assist anyone who wishes to confide in us and asks for counsel. We ought to make ourselves available because a **wise word can truly be a precious help**! But we shouldn't take this responsibility lightly.

First, we must turn to our perfect advisor: **the Holy Spirit**.

Even on the Bus

Pope Francis realizes the importance of the gift of "counsel." On May 7, 2014, the Holy Father taught the crowds gathered in Saint Peter's Square. He said that the gift of counsel enables us to make choices that are in union with God and the Gospel. Acknowledging that the Spirit helps us grow interiorly, positively, and with others, Pope Francis

Counsel is one of the gifts of the Holy Spirit we receive with the sacrament of Confirmation. It is important that we ask for this gift ourselves first, and then for those who are close to us.

said that the gift of counsel keeps us from becoming self-centered and makes it possible for us to live in community.

The Holy Father shared that he asks for this gift himself every day and he encourages us to do the same. He advised us to pray and make time for the Holy Spirit to show us what to do. He added that we can pray everywhere—even on the bus or the streets. Prayer, he said, is something we must never forget, and it's possible to pray without anyone ever knowing what we are doing.

Notebook

✓ Read this selection from the Bible in which King Solomon asks God for a "docile," or open and childlike, heart.

"At Gibeon the Lord appeared to Solomon in a dream by night; and God said, 'Ask what I should give you.' And Solomon said, 'You have shown great and steadfast love to your servant my father, David, because he walked before you in faithfulness, in righteousness, and in uprightness of heart toward you; and you have kept for him this great and steadfast love, and have given him a son to sit on his throne today. And now, O Lord my God, you have made your servant king in place of my father, David, although I am only a little child; I do not know how to go out or come in. And your servant is in the midst of the people whom you have chosen, a great people, so numerous they cannot be numbered or counted. Give your servant therefore an understanding mind to govern your people, able to discern between good and evil; for who can govern this, your great people?'

"It pleased the Lord that Solomon has asked this. God said to him, 'Because you have asked this, and have not asked for yourself long life or riches, or for the life of your enemies, but have asked for yourself understanding to discern what is right, I now do according to your word. Indeed I give you a wise and discerning mind; no one like you has been before you and no one like you shall arise after you. I give you also what you have not asked, both riches and honor all your life; no other king shall compare with you.'"

1 Kings 3:5–13

✓ Who are the people you trust and turn to for counsel about an important decision or puzzling question? Write their names on a sheet of paper, thank God for their presence in your life, and pray that the Holy Spirit will guide them.

Spiritual Works of Mercy

2. Instruct the Ignorant

"All scripture is inspired by God and is useful for teaching, for reproof, for correction, and for training in righteousness."

2 Tim 3:16

2nd Who Doesn't Know?

The "'ignorant" are "people who do not know" or "people who are not learned" because they do not have an education.

This spiritual work of mercy reminds us of the need to be instructed and informed.

It is important for us to have knowledge in order to be good citizens and to become free and responsible people who are able to contribute to our society. It takes learning to make our talents and gifts—which each of us has received—fruitful, so that we can find solutions and new paths, and encounter the future while helping others and making the world a better place.

It is urgent that the leaders of all nations do their part so that every child can go to school and learn. Although the right to education is recognized by some, today sixty-one million primary school-age children do not go to school: this means one out of every ten children

The Nobel Prize for Peace

Read this brief excerpt from a speech by Malala Yousafzai made to the United Nations in 2013.

Taliban terrorists tried to kill this sixteen-year-old Afghani girl in 2012 because she spoke out against their forbidding girls to go to school. She was awarded the Nobel Prize for Peace in 2014.

"Dear brothers and sisters, we want schools, and instruction, and a bright future for every child. We will continue our journey toward the destination of peace and education. No one can stop us. We will raise our voices for our rights and our voices will carry change. We believe in the strength of our words. Our words can change the world, because we are all together, united for the cause of education.

in the world! Many young people are required to **work** (over 200 million in the world) or **live in a war zone** (it is estimated that twenty-eight million children live in areas where there is armed conflict). The most disadvantaged remain the children who live in the poorest regions. Many of them become mothers at too young an age, or

need to take care of their homes and their siblings without having had any access to basic instruction. In every part of the world both lay and religious Christians build schools, teach, and train local teachers. They freely welcome children so that even the poorest can receive a basic education, which allows them to have new perspectives and possibilities.

"And if we want to reach our objective, we seek to arm ourselves with the weapon of knowledge and the shield of unity and solidarity.

"Dear brothers and sisters, we must not forget that millions of people suffer poverty, injustice, and ignorance. We must not forget that millions of children are not allowed to attend their schools. We must not forget that our brothers and sisters are waiting for a bright future of peace.

"Therefore let us seek to lead a glorious fight against illiteracy, poverty, and terrorism; we must wield books and pens because they are the most powerful weapons. A child, a teacher, a book, and a pen can change the world. Education is the only solution. Education is the first thing."

Notebook

✓ Today we watch a movie!
Find the documentary film titled, "On the Way to School" by the French director, Pascal Plisson. Ask your parents or teacher to check it out of the library or download it. This movie tells the story of how four children between the ages of eleven and thirteen years old, in four remote places, walk for hours every day and risk their lives just to attend school. These kids, who are around your age, are happy to go to school because they know that education is their greatest opportunity. They take full advantage of what is open to them and do not give up despite dangers, hardships, and obstacles.

✓ Read the words of Saint Marguerite Bourgeoys, a French religious sister who established the first school in present day Montreal:

> "Teaching is the work most suited to draw the graces of God if it is done with purity of intention, without distinction between the poor and the rich, between relatives and friends and strangers, between the pretty and the ugly, the gentle and the grumblers . . ."

How can you help a classmate or younger sibling learn a subject they are struggling with?

✓ Together with your family, religious education group, or parish, find out about associations that offer child sponsorships. This type of help is aimed at providing medical and educational help to thousands of children all over the world. It would be beautiful to be able to contribute so that faraway "brothers" or "sisters" can get an education and have a better chance to improve their condition, as well as that of their family and their community.

Spiritual Works of Mercy

3. Admonish the Sinner

> "Hear, O my people,
> while I admonish you;
> O Israel, if you would
> but listen to me!"
>
> Ps 81:8

41

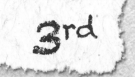

I Care

"Admonish" means "to advise, to encourage a person, or to warn against danger." Admonishing sinners, the third spiritual work of mercy, is about **taking care of one another** and not turning a blind eye if we see someone close to us take the wrong road. It's not easy because we must be careful not to express condemnation or judgment. A warning must be given **with love** and for the good of the person. And, we must always keep in mind that we are sinners, too. Still it is an important work of mercy; true friends help each other to be good. Furthermore, warning others about danger is an act of true affection.

The Prophet Who Spoke the Truth to His King

In the Bible, we find the story of King David, who had all kinds of riches as well as numerous wives. Still, it was not enough for him. David coveted the wife of Uriah the soldier. In order to take her for himself, he had Uriah killed. The Lord then sent the prophet Nathan to speak to King David and tell him that he had done evil and left the right path. Nathan told a story to help the king understand his error and become aware of his sin. David repented and asked God to forgive him.

"But the thing that David had done displeased the LORD, and the LORD sent Nathan to David. He came to him, and said to him,

Our Eyes First

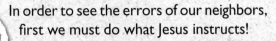

In order to see the errors of our neighbors, first we must do what Jesus instructs!

"Jesus also told them a parable: 'Can a blind person guide a blind person? Will not both fall into a pit? A disciple is not above the teacher, but everyone who is fully qualified will be like the teacher. Why do you see the speck in your neighbor's eye, but do not notice the log in your own eye? Or how can you say to your neighbor, 'Friend, let me take out the speck in your eye,' when you yourself do not see the log in your own eye? You hypocrite, first take the log out of your own eye, and then you will see clearly to take the speck out of your neighbor's eye'" (Lk 6:39–42).

'There were two men in a certain city, the one rich and the other poor. The rich man had very many flocks and herds; but the poor man had nothing but one little ewe lamb, which he had bought. He brought it up, and it grew up with him and with his children; it used to eat of his meager fare, and drink of his cup, and lie in his bosom, and it was like a daughter to him. Now there came a traveler to the rich man, and he was loath to take one of his own flock or herd to prepare for the wayfarer who had come to him, but he took the poor man's lamb, and prepared that for the guest who had come to him.' Then David's anger was greatly kindled against the man. He said to Nathan, 'As the LORD lives, the man who has done this deserves to die; he shall restore the lamb fourfold, because he did this thing and because he had no pity.'

"Nathan said to David, 'You are the man!'" (2 Sam 12:1–7).

Notebook

✓ Have you ever admonished someone who was doing something wrong?

When you are with a friend who makes a mistake or commits a sin, do you ignore it, or do you intervene?

Is it easy to defend what you know is right?

When you see someone committing a grave sin, do you think that it is none of your business?

✓ Read this prayer of Saint Faustina Kowalska as she speaks of God's mercy for sinners. Learn to pray for those who have sinned and to remember in prayer those who have fallen away from what is good.

"O God of great mercy, you sent us your only Son as the greatest demonstration of limitless love and mercy. You do not reject sinners. Rather, you have opened to them the treasure of your infinite mercy, so that they can draw not only justification but an abundance of every holiness to which souls can reach. Father of great mercy, I desire that all hearts would trust in your infinite mercy."

Saint Faustina Kowalska

Spiritual Works of Mercy

4. Comfort the Afflicted

"As a mother comforts her child, so I will comfort you."

Is 66:13

Like a Mother

The book of Isaiah in the Bible presents a beautiful image of God to us. The prophet writes that **God consoles his people** like a loving mother consoles her child.

In this tender image, God bends down to us and makes us feel how near he is to us; he raises us when we fall; he dries our tears; he reassures us of his love.

In another passage, the prophet Isaiah speaks to those who are returning from exile about how God leads them like a shepherd, with care and attention, respecting all the sheep and

A Consoling Testimony

As Christians, we are called to bring God's consolation to the world. Pope Francis reminds us that we cannot give what we ourselves have not experienced. In order to know God's love personally, the Holy Father encourages us to listen to God's word, pray silently in his presence, and encounter him in both the Eucharist and in the sacrament of Reconciliation. He emphasized the need for us to witness to the Lord's mercy and tenderness today—to jolt those who have given up, revive the discouraged, and light a flame of hope.

carrying in his arms those who struggle: "He will feed his flock like a shepherd; he will gather the lambs in his arms, and carry them . . . , and gently lead the mother sheep" (Is 40:11). This is how God comes to comfort and console us: with tenderness. God comes lovingly to raise us, to free us from our prisons, and to carry us home again. This work of mercy asks us to do the same for our neighbor.

How can we comfort those who suffer? First of all, we need to look around us and see the lives of our neighbors with new eyes. We can learn to recognize sadness and the **need for comfort**, the need to speak to someone who will listen and to receive a word of encouragement and hope. When we are truly aware of those who are near us, then we can console and comfort them. We can **be present with tenderness**, listen with love, and give hope to our neighbor.

Remember, too, that Jesus is quick to give us his Spirit, which he also called "the Comforter." Therefore, we can ask God to comfort us as well as our neighbors with this spirit of love that heals our hurts, consoles us, and encourages us to continue on the path of faith.

Our lives are filled with situations in which we need comfort and consolation. Think about people who are oppressed, suffer injustice or abuse, or those who are slaves to money, power, and worldly success. Pope Francis calls us to console all our brothers and sisters and tell them that only God can eliminate what causes them to experience spiritual crisis and lose sight of the meaning of their lives.

Notebook

✓ Read the words below. They come from a beautiful prayer for Pentecost and can help you to know and feel God's presence near you. Copy this prayer and give it to someone you know who needs the comfort of knowing that God does not abandon anyone and is quick to send his Holy Spirit, the perfect "Consoler."

> Come, Holy Spirit,
> send forth from heaven
> the rays of your light.
> Come, father of the poor;
> come, giver of gifts;
> come, light of our hearts.
> Come, O most perfect Comforter,
> sweet guest of souls,
> sweetest relief, who is
> in labor, rest,
> in heat, coolness,
> in tears, comfort.

✓ Reflect on this work of mercy. Place an X next to the ways you have already comforted someone on the list below. You have . . .

☹ 😐 😀

☐ ☐ ☐ Consoled a friend

☐ ☐ ☐ Used the words of the Gospel to encourage someone

☐ ☐ ☐ Prayed for those who are sad or being tested

☐ ☐ ☐ Expressed my closeness and support with gestures or words

☐ ☐ ☐ Felt the pain of others

☐ ☐ ☐ Found a way to bring hope to those who suffer

Now circle one or two things on the list that you will commit to doing today.

Spiritual Works of Mercy

5. Forgive Offenses Willingly

"But I say to you, love your enemies and pray for those who persecute you, so that you may be children of your Father in heaven; for he makes his sun rise on the evil and on the good, and sends rain on the righteous and on the un- righteous. For if you love those who love you, what reward do you have?"

Mt 5:44–46

Receive, Give

Jesus' teaching urges us to **be like God**. In fact Jesus says, "Be merciful, just as your Father is merciful. Do not judge, and you will not be judged; do not condemn, and you will not be condemned. Forgive, and you will be forgiven . . ." (Lk 6:36–37).

As God's children we are called to forgive and to be like God who is full of mercy.

The fifth spiritual work of mercy highlights one of the most important of Jesus' teachings: loving one's enemies by **forgiving those who have offended us.**

Every time we pray the Our Father, we ask God to "forgive us our trespasses as we forgive those who trespass against us." With this phrase we ask God to forgive us for what we have done and what we have failed to do. We also tell God, however, that we will do the same by forgiving our neighbors when they harm us. The forgiveness we receive from God is a gift that we ought to be quick to pass on to our neighbor. We cannot keep forgiveness to ourselves.

The Exact Number

In the Gospels, Peter asked Jesus an important question. The answer teaches us how God wants men and women to forgive each other.

"Then Peter came and said to him, 'Lord, if another member of the church sins against me, how often should I forgive? As many as seven times?' Jesus said to him, 'Not seven times, but, I tell you, seventy-seven times'". (Mt 18:21–22).

Peter was Jesus' disciple and had heard him preach. He knew that

The Big News

Pope Francis commented on a passage of the Bible that speaks about loving one's enemies. He said that giving one's self, even to those who wish us ill or do us wrong—even to our enemies—is what is new about the Gospel. Recognizing that this is not easy to do, the Holy Father challenged us to follow Jesus' example. He further reminded us that we are called to live the words we say every day in the Our Father: "forgive us as we forgive others." After all, if we are not willing to forgive, how can any of us ask our Heavenly Father, "Will you forgive me?"

forgiveness is basic to Jesus' teachings. So he thought of a number that seemed to him to be reasonably large: **seven**. In fact, in the time and culture of Jesus' people, the number seven symbolized completeness. (An example of this is the seven days of Creation.)

Still, Jesus responded to Peter by giving him an unthinkable and astonishing number! **Jesus put Peter off balance and invited him to think of forgiveness the way God himself wants it to be.** Jesus teaches us to forgive from the heart—without counting our neighbors' offenses and without putting limits on the possibility of beginning anew.

Notebook

V Read the following two reflections on the forgiveness we ask for in the Our Father.

"The Lord taught us to pray for our trespasses and our sins (. . .). Then he clearly added a law tying us to a pact and a sure promise. We can ask that our sins be forgiven, but only in the measure with which we forgive those who trespass against us. We cannot receive what we ask for our sins if we haven't reached out in the same way to those who are in debt to us."

Saint Cyprian

"Forgive our trespasses as we forgive those who trespass against us. We seek to say these words every day with a sincere heart and to put into practice what we say. And we remember: it is a solemn pact, a promise that engages us, and it's an agreement that we make with God."

Saint Augustine

V Are you aware of this "pact" or agreement that God makes with you?

V Do you try to give others the kind of forgiveness you ask for yourself?

Spiritual Work of Mercy

6. Bear Wrongs Patiently

"Bear with one another and, if anyone has a complaint against another, forgive each other."

Col 3:13

6th Weight in Gold!

This work of mercy invites us all to recognize that sometimes we lack patience. It asks us to learn how to bear with our neighbors and with their imperfections.

Saint Bernard said that if a Christian did not have a person to annoy him, he should go out and find one and then pay them their weight in gold! Why? Because that person teaches us how to exercise **patience and meekness**. These are two important virtues for anyone who wants to follow Christ. It is Jesus, after all, who gives us the example. If we think about his years of ministry, we see that Jesus welcomed everyone and answered their questions—even questions from people who were trying to get him into trouble. Jesus listened to the sick, welcomed children who made noise, cared for strangers, and ate with sinners. He did not reject anyone.

A Light Yoke

Sometimes we feel the "weight" of our neighbors' imperfections. Using the word "bear" in naming the sixth work of mercy communicates the idea of carrying a load. Jesus once used the image of farm equipment to illustrate what it was like to follow him. A yoke is a very heavy wooden board that holds a pair of oxen together and harnesses them to a plow.

"Jesus said, 'Come to me, all of you that are weary and are carrying heavy burdens, and I will give you rest. Take my yoke upon you and learn from me; for I am gentle and humble in heart. . . . For my yoke is easy, and my burden is light'" (Mt 11:28–30).

54

Patience, a Fruit of the Holy Spirit

The fruits of the Holy Spirit are qualities that are formed in us by grace. The tradition of the Church numbers twelve of them, and Saint Paul lists nine in his Letter to the Galatians. Among these gifts are joy, peace, goodness, faithfulness, and patience. It is beautiful to think that when we are patient with a neighbor, we are allowing the work of the Holy Spirit to grow in us.

Jesus, gentle and humble of heart, tells us that if we patiently accept each others' limitations, and we learn to be humble like he is, we will find the "yoke" of following him "light" and "sweet."

It's not magic! Jesus himself carries this yoke—one that seems to be heavy—with us. He is at our side and will not leave us alone when we choose to do good and to love our neighbor. Jesus loved each one of us to the end and carried the heaviest yoke, the cross. Still, it didn't crush him. Jesus' love, his total gift, conquered death with the resurrection.

In the New Testament we can read this blessing: "May the Lord direct your hearts to the love of God and to the steadfastness of Christ" (2 Thess 3:5).

Notebook

✓ Have you ever been annoyed or bothered by someone? Think of your friends, classmates, teammates, religious education group, and family members. Have you ever lost your patience with one of them?

If you reflect on this work of mercy, can you begin to look at them with different eyes?

✓ Read Saint Paul's beautiful words about love. Underline the part that you like most, the one you feel is most directed to you in this moment.

> "Love is patient; love is kind;
> love is not envious or boastful
> or arrogant or rude.
> It does not insist on its own way;
> it is not irritable or resentful;
> it does not rejoice in wrongdoing,
> but rejoices in the truth.
> It bears all things,
> believes all things,
> hopes all things,
> endures all things.
> Love never ends."
>
> 1 Corinthians 13:4-8

Spiritual Works of Mercy

7. Pray for the Living and the Dead

*Eternal rest
grant unto them, O Lord,
and let perpetual light
shine upon them.
May they rest in peace.
Amen.*

7th

Prayer, a Work of Mercy

The last spiritual work of mercy is praying for the living and the dead, that is, for all men and women. With prayer Christians can "intercede" and bring the sufferings, joys, needs, and hopes of our brothers and sisters to God.

Pope Saint John Paul II wrote that God has entrusted all of us to one another.

Isn't this bond amazing? Praying for our neighbor makes us closer to God *and* closer to the brother or sister we are caring for. When we understand this, then prayer reveals itself to us as a network of love that unites us. Prayer is an *alliance*, a tie between us and God through Jesus; it is a true communion and a living relationship between God and his children.

Praying for Everyone

It is "good and acceptable" in God's eyes when we pray for everyone. This is because God loves all people and sent Jesus, his Son, so that all may be saved.

"First of all, then, I urge that supplications, prayers, intercessions, and thanksgivings be made for everyone. . . . This is right and is acceptable in the sight of God our Savior, who desires everyone to be saved and to come to the knowledge of the truth. For

I Am in Peace

"But the souls of the righteous are in the hand of God, and no torment will ever touch them. In the eyes of the foolish they seem to have died, and their departure was thought to be a disaster, and their going from us to be their destruction; but they are at peace . . . and the faithful will abide with him in love, because grace and mercy are upon his holy ones, and he watches over his elect" (Wis 3:1–3, 9).

Loved ones who have died do not disappear into thin air but "live in God" and remain bound to us through prayer, above all when we participate in the celebration of the Holy Eucharist. When we pray for the deceased, we affirm the faith that reminds us that physical death is not the end of life.

When we pray for those who have died, we commend them to God's mercy. With the priest's words in the First Eucharistic Prayer we ask, **"Grant them, O Lord, we pray, and all who sleep in Christ, a place of refreshment, light, and peace."**

there is one God; there is also one mediator between God and humankind, Christ Jesus, himself human, who gave himself a ransom for all" (1 Tim 2:1–6).

Notebook

✓ Prayer does not take the place of doing, acting, and making choices. Saint Ignatius of Loyola wrote, "Pray as if everything depends on God and work as if everything depends on you."
What does this mean? If you pray for a friend, a family member, or another person you know, you also ought to be ready to do your part to personally help them.

✓ As we reach the end of our study on the spiritual works of mercy, read the prayer below. Pray that your life may truly become an "instrument" of God's peace and goodness for all people.

"O Lord, make me an instrument of your peace.
Where there is hatred, let me bring your love.
Where there is injury, may I bring pardon.
Where there is discord, may I bring unity.
Where there is doubt, may I bring faith.
Where there is error, may I bring truth.
Where there is despair, may I bring hope.
Where there is sadness, may I bring joy.
Where there is darkness, may I bring light.
O Master, grant that I may not so much seek
to be consoled, as to console;
to be understood, as to understand;
to be loved, as to love.
Because it is in giving that we receive,
in forgiving that we are forgiven,
in dying that we are born to eternal life."

Saint Francis of Assisi

Come, O Blessed of My Father!

Finally we re-read Jesus' words in Matthew's Gospel. "Every time that you did these things to even one of these my brothers, you did it to me."

"When the Son of Man comes in his glory, and all the angels with him, then he will sit on the throne of his glory. All the nations will be gathered before him, and he will separate people one from another as a shepherd separates the sheep from the goats, and he will put the sheep at his right hand and the goats at the left. Then the king will say to those at his right hand, 'Come you that are blessed by my Father, inherit the kingdom prepared for you from the foundation of the world; for I was hungry and you gave me food, I was thirsty and you gave me something to drink, I was a stranger and you welcomed me, I was naked and you gave me clothing, I was sick and you took care of me, I was in prison and you visited me.' Then the righteous will answer him, 'Lord, when was it that we saw you hungry and gave you food, or thirsty and gave you something to drink? And when was it that we saw you a stranger and welcomed you, or naked and gave you clothing? And when was it that we saw you sick or in prison and we visited you?' And the king will answer them, 'Truly I tell you, just as you did it to one of the least of these who are members of my family, you did it to me.' Then he will say to those at his left hand, 'You that are accursed, depart from me into the eternal fire prepared for the devil and his angels; for I was hungry and you gave me no food, I was thirsty and you gave me nothing to drink, I was a stranger and you did not welcome me, naked and you did not give me clothing, sick and in prison and you did not visit me.' Then they also will answer, 'Lord, when was it that we saw you hungry or thirsty or a stranger or naked or sick or in prison and did not take care of you?' Then he will answer them, 'Truly I tell you, just as you did not do it to one of the least of these, you did not do it to me.'"

Matthew 25:31–45

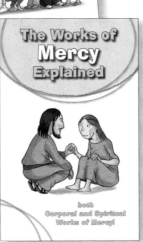